A souvenir guide

Nuffield Place

Oxfordshire

CW00351227

L 2
a
T 4
6
8 The gift of giving
10 Lord and Lady Nuffield

The House   12
14 The Hall
14 The Drawing Room
16 The Dining Room
18 The Sitting Room
20 The Landing
20 The Single Guest Bedroom
20 Lady Nuffield's Bedroom
22 The Sun Room
22 Lord Nuffield's Bedroom
24 The bathrooms
24 Lady Nuffield's Sewing Room
26 The Double Guest Bedroom

The Garden   28

Staff at Nuffield   32

National Trust

Lord Nuffield and his Home

There is another William Morris. Not the William Morris of Arts and Crafts fame treasured for his ever-so-English wallpapers, fabrics and furniture, but the one – equally, if not more, important – to whom we owe the Morris Minor and other much-loved British cars.

William Morris, later known as Lord Nuffield, brought cheap motoring to Britain, by introducing mass production processes and relying on economies of scale. But his legacy stretches beyond his pioneering work with cars. As one of the greatest philanthropists of the 20th century, he helped many causes, the most important of which is anaesthetics. We have him to thank for pain-free operations.

Nuffield Place

Nuffield Place was Lord Nuffield's home from 1933 until his death in 1963. Originally named Merrow Mount, the house was designed by Oswald Partridge Milne in 1914 for Sir John Bowring Wimble, a shipping magnate and

Above This 1960 photograph of Nuffield Place shows the house and garden as they looked just a few years before Lord Nuffield's death

Left 'Did you realise that two car ownership as provided by Morris is actually more economical than one big car?'. Morris cars became well known for their affordability

chairman of C. T. Bowring (Insurance) Ltd. Milne was a pupil of the great British architect Sir Edwin Lutyens and, in its understated Arts and Crafts-style exterior, the design owes much to the latter. This was Milne's third commission in the parish, having previously completed Huntercombe Golf clubhouse and Huntercombe Hall. Milne is known for having designed Coleton Fishacre, the elegant Devon home of Rupert D'Oyly Carte, now also in the care of the National Trust.

New owners

After Sir John Wimble died, his widow sold the house in 1933 to William Morris, who at the time was living in part of Huntercombe Golf Club's converted clubhouse down the road. Having just been raised to the peerage, William took his title from the village and renamed his new home Nuffield Place.

He and his wife Elizabeth altered the house, enlarging the sitting and dining rooms, adding a new kitchen and billiard room, creating a first-floor veranda, installing central heating and modernising the bathrooms. But this four-bedroom house was hardly the typical home of a millionaire – and while it gained in comfort and practicality, it never became lavish. That Morris employed a local builder rather than an architect for the alterations says something about his frugal nature.

Authentic décor

Rather than being decorated with up-to-the-minute and opulent Art Deco furnishings, Nuffield Place reflects the more mainstream tastes of the 1930s. Good-qualit reproduction furniture mixes with a sprinkli of antiques; flower paintings combine with tapestries and Oriental carpets, adding touches of colour and pattern. The general feel is one of homeliness and comfort rather than opulence and display.

Far from the madding crowd

Though this was their only home, Nuffield Place was much like a private weekend retreat. Here Lord Nuffield could escape the pressures of work and recharge his batteries in the company of his wife and close friends.

Final bequest

On Lord Nuffield's death in 1963, Nuffield Place was bequeathed to Nuffield College (see page 9). The College looked after the house and its contents until 2012, when it gave Nuffield Place to the National Trust.

Above Lord and Lady Nuffield spent most evenings in their cosy Sitting Room

Below Miniatures of Lord and Lady Nuffield

The Modest Millionaire

From relatively humble beginnings, William Morris became the most famous industrialist of his age and one of the greatest philanthropists of the 20th century.

Below left **Lord Nuffield, 1930s**

Below **Cars and drivers in front of the Morris Garage in the early 1900s; William Morris is mid-right**

Inauspicious start

William Morris was born on 10 October 1877 in Worcester and moved to Oxford with his family when he was three. His father, Frederick Morris, worked as a bailiff on his father-in-law's farm until severe asthma attacks forced him to take on clerical jobs to support a family of seven, of whom William, or Will as he was known, was the eldest.

In order to help his father, William left school at 14 and started working as an apprentice in an Oxford bicycle shop. He was not able to pursue his goal of becoming a surgeon, but this thwarted childhood dream never stood in the way of his ambition. After just a year Morris asked for a pay rise; when the request was refused he promptly set up his own business.

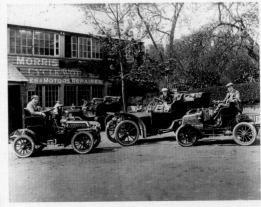

Budding entrepreneur

Aged 16 and with capital of just £4, Morris started his own bicycle-repair business in a shed at the back of his parents' home. Soon afterwards, he began designing custom-built bicycles, which gained a reputation for reliability and good value. By 1901 Morris had acquired a shop on Oxford's High Street and by 1903 he was manufacturing motorcycles. Morris's boundless nervous energy and keen business sense brought rapid success and formed the basis for his expanding fortunes.

Onwards and upwards

In 1909, Morris set up the Morris Garage on Oxford's Longwall Street, where he started selling, hiring and repairing cars. By 1913, sales had quadrupled and new showrooms were acquired on Queen Street.

'My so-called apprenticeship was a complete myth. I was never taught anything.'

Lord Nuffield

The Guv'nor

During his Longwall Garage days, Morris was affectionately called Uncle by his little band of employees. As his business grew, he became known, more grandly, as the Guv'nor. Morris looked for loyalty from his staff and had a reputation for being fair, straightforward and decisive. He also expected a lot, but was always aware of how much he owed to his staff. As his career progressed and he became world famous, Morris was described as the 'Henry Ford of England'.

Above left **William Morris** (left) repairing a bicycle

Above right **Lord Nuffield** was never driven by fame or glory, as this obituary highlights

Motoring ahead

The first Morris car

A practical man with a passion for engineering, Morris was fascinated by how things were made. So from the selling, hiring and repairing of cars, it was only natural that he should move to their actual assembly. In August 1912, he registered a new company, WRM Motors Ltd., for the manufacture of cars. Using bought-in components, including a small 10-horsepower four-cylinder side-valve engine made by the firm of White & Poppe in Coventry, he created his first car in 1913.

"That's it!
... the car with the lowest upkeep costs

I'm going to have a

MORRIS"

Ⓝ NUFFIELD PRODUCT

MORRIS MOTORS LTD · COWLEY · OXFORD

C.35H

Above Assembly line workers at the Morris Motors factory at Cowley, 1930

Left An early Morris advert

Mass appeal

Affordable and easy to maintain, the two-seater Morris Oxford was aimed at the popular market and competitively priced at £175. It was so appealing that London dealer Gordon Stewart ordered 400 cars from blueprints alone. Once on the road, the car earned its nickname, the Bullnose, thanks to its distinctive bullet-nosed radiator. Even the unusual placement of the accelerator pedal in the middle did not stop it from becoming the bestselling car in Britain in the 1920s.

By 1914, Morris had acquired larger premises in Cowley on the outskirts of Oxford. There he started producing a second car, the Morris Cowley, made entirely from American components. But as war broke out car production ground to a halt and Morris joined the war effort, producing a range of military products. Although these made him little money, the experience taught him much about mass-production, one of the keys to his post-war success.

Secrets of success

It was during the 1920s that Morris established himself as one the main players in the burgeoning car industry. By 1923 he was producing more than 20,000 cars a year at extremely competitive prices. By 1925 sales of the Bullnose represented an astonishing 45 per cent of the British market.

Focusing on economies of scale, Morris drove down suppliers' prices in exchange for promises of large orders. This was a risky strategy, as it involved committing to large-scale production, but it paid off. So much so that Morris soon acquired additional factories in Abingdon, Birmingham and Swindon and took over the ownership of some of his suppliers.

Backed up by imaginative advertising, the Morris brand became synonymous with reliability, comfort and competitive prices. Morris introduced hire purchase schemes during the 1920s, which helped attract even more customers. In 1925 the *Morris Owner* magazine was launched. Each issue boasted specially commissioned full-colour cover artwork, helpful articles and motor-related adverts. While reinforcing the brand, it also encouraged customer loyalty. So too did innovations in customer service, such as fixed prices for servicing dispensed from Morris dealerships across the country.

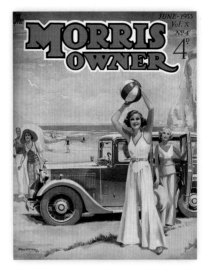
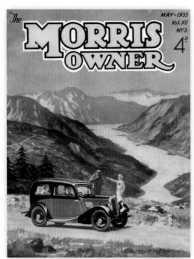
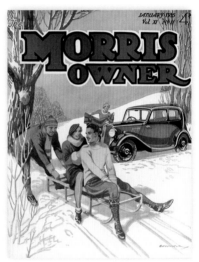
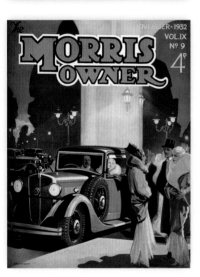

'There's nothing annoys me more than when anyone calls me lucky. The man who calls you lucky you'll generally find has missed any opportunity that came along.'

Lord Nuffield

Above Selection of *Morris Owner* magazine covers from the 1920s and 1930s. From the delights of beach and touring holidays to the luxury of evening parties, the magazine was clearly 'selling the dream'

The gift of giving

Lord Nuffield was never extravagant with his money, even when at the height of his career he was reputedly earning £2,000 a day. Questioned about his riches, he replied: 'Well, you can only wear one suit at a time.' Naturally frugal and with no children of his own, he gave away much of his vast fortune to good causes. His was a life of two careers: one as an industrialist, the other as a philanthropist.

In total he donated £30 million, the equivalent of £700 million today. Lord Nuffield took his charitable work very seriously, stating that 'the worry which comes from giving is very great'.

His passion for medicine, coupled with his strong sense of social justice, informed his choice of donations, which were carefully considered and often the result of discussions with his wife Elizabeth.

Wealth well-given

Nuffield started making donations in the 1920s. One of his earliest large benefactions was a £10,000 grant to help parents visit their children in borstals. In 1927, he started giving large sums to hospitals, particularly in those areas where he had factories, such as Birmingham and Oxford.

In 1936, he floated much of his ordinary stock, giving him access to yet more funds. In that same year and with capital of £2 million, he set up a Trust for Special Areas to help regions severely affected by the Great Depression. The following year he gave

Acts of kindness

During the war, Lord Nuffield gave away free cigarettes for the troops and sanitary towels for women. He also provided sun lamps to factory workers, to help make up for the lack of sunlight. After a particularly rough sea journey, Nuffield considered that he had been so well looked after by his cabin steward that he gave him a Morris car as a tip. But while he believed in helping people, he also thought that a person should make his or her own way in life, as he had done.

> 'It is more difficult to give money than to make it.'
>
> Lord Nuffield

Above Lord Nuffield on his 62nd birthday putting a £100,000 cheque into a nurse's collecting box at the Mansion House, 10 October 1939

Left One of Lord Nuffield's many obituaries. He was as passionate about philanthropy as he was about the manufacturing and selling of cars

£50,000 towards the expansion of the Sea Cadet Corps.

Lord Nuffield's donations are far too numerous to list individually – suffice to say that his desire to relieve the sick, the crippled and the poor and to alleviate social injustice drove much of his philanthropy.

His gift-giving culminated in the establishment of the following Oxford-based foundations: the Nuffield Orthopaedic Centre (1931), the Nuffield Institute for Medical Research (1936), Nuffield College (1937) and the Nuffield Foundation (1943). Set up with a capital of about £10 million to provide medical and social relief, the Nuffield Foundation was to become a major educational grant-giving body from the 1950s onwards. His legacies had great impact in the fields of social science, anaesthetics and orthopaedics. Elizabeth also made her mark, establishing the Elizabeth Nuffield Educational Fund in 1956, to help women develop their career prospects through education.

Lord and Lady Nuffield

Lord Nuffield, the man

Of medium height and build, Lord Nuffield had piercing blue eyes and his voice had a distinctive Oxfordshire burr. Although personable, he was deeply reserved and on occasion distant. Worry, nervous energy, and a strong competitive streak are what drove him. A light sleeper, he would often 'worry out' a problem in the middle of the night. As many of the portraits and photographs of him demonstrate, he was also a very keen smoker.

More than meets the eye

Lord Nuffield's public persona was, however, somewhat removed from his private personality. At home and in the company of close friends, he was relaxed, enjoyed a good joke and a sing-song and, as we shall see, even indulged in a spot of dressing up.

'Without worry, you never get anywhere.'

Lord Nuffield

Pomp and ceremony

Lord and Lady Nuffield were not ones to spend excessive amounts of money on clothes, but they made an exception for the Coronation Ceremony of George VI and Queen Elizabeth on 12 May 1937. Their robes of velvet, ermine and white satin are truly sumptuous. The two rows of ermine on Lord Nuffield's cape signify his standing as a Baron.

Lord and Lady Nuffield
at Nuffield Place

Public honours

Thanks to his benefactions and hard work, Lord Nuffield was awarded two peerages and granted many academic, civic, colonial and medical honours. Listed below are the most important.

1917 OBE
1929 Baronet, becoming Sir William Morris
1934 Baron Nuffield
1938 Viscount Nuffield
1939 Fellow of the Royal Society
1941 GBE
1948 Fellow of the Royal College of Surgeons
1958 Companion of Honour

Lady Nuffield

Married in 1903, William Morris and Elizabeth Anstey (1884–1959) met through a shared love of cycling. In their youth, they would often cycle from Oxford to Wales or the West Country and back in a weekend.

Like her husband, Elizabeth was careful with money. Her one extravagance was travel. While Lord Nuffield enjoyed his winter cruises (see page 13), she set off for the Riviera. At home, she enjoyed gardening, sewing, jam making and bottling, walking, and the company of her Scottie dogs.

A childless union

No one knows why the couple never had children, but Lord Nuffield admitted that he would have given away all his millions for a child of his own. There is, however, no doubt that Lord and Lady Nuffield's marriage was a successful one.

'After Lady Nuffield died he became a lonely man and he began to lose interest in everything.'

Carl Kingerlee,
Lord Nuffield's private secretary

The House

As his home reveals, Lord Nuffield was a man who combined financial prudence and practicality with a sense of fun.

As you step inside, you might be transported back to the home of your parents or grandparents. There is a sense of nostalgia, of the not-so-distant past, which makes Nuffield Place irresistibly engaging and raises it beyond being a monument to a great man. It is a time capsule of a lost era – a time when people used to sit and listen to records or the wireless and indulge in afternoon tea.

Above Lord Nuffield's armorial bearings

Opposite A collection of walking sticks, golf clubs and umbrellas in the Billiard Room

Right This unusual contraption, known as an electric exercise horse, was specially designed for Lord Nuffield

Below right A corner of the Billiard Room

The Billiard Room

Designed as a comfortable space for Lord Nuffield and his male guests, the Billiard Room was added to the house in 1933. Its wood panelling and floor not only create a feeling of richness and warmth but also complement the Art Deco burr walnut cocktail cabinet and the billiard table itself.

Somewhat unexpected is the electric exercise horse. Made at the Morris car factory for Lord Nuffield, this unusual item is like a modern-day exercise bike – except that this one has just two speeds: gallop and trot. Lord Nuffield kept the contraption at his office in Cowley and apparently used it on a daily basis.

Hole in one
Lord Nuffield was a keen golfer, as indicated by the golf clubs in the umbrella stand. Every day he would go to Huntercombe Golf Club with his dogs, hit a ball or two and then come back. On weekends he would play a full round, either with his wife or with friends.

Foiled…
The newspaper cuttings in this room relate to the attempted kidnap of Lord Nuffield in 1938. Two men, Thornton and Ramsden, planned to confront him at gunpoint in his office and detain him until a £10,000 ransom had been paid. Ramsden got cold feet and informed the police, who told him to carry on as planned. Thornton was caught on his way to Lord Nuffield's office and subsequently sentenced to seven years' penal service. A reporter from the *Daily Sketch* wrote on 25 May 1938: 'In spite of the experience, Lord Nuffield seemed quite composed and made very little of the affair.'

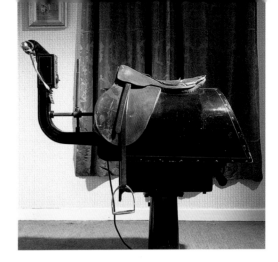

All hands on deck
On the end wall is a shield featuring a deck quoit, which Lord Nuffield used during one of his many sea voyages. His annual sea journeys started in 1927–8; they were a means of developing trade and keeping in touch with dealers. But although he worked while on shore, he used his time at sea to relax and perfect his considerable skills at deck tennis.

Behind the symbols
Lord Nuffield's armorial bearings include beavers (symbolising hard work), pears (for the city of Worcester, where he was born) and an ox (for Oxford). The scales go with his motto *Fiat Justitia* ('Be Just'), while the bunches of speedwell flowers are an allusion to the best way to enjoy a journey by motor car.

The Hall
The Drawing Room

The Hall

Despite appearances all the furniture in the Hall is reproduction, including the four William and Mary-style chairs with tapestry seats. Here again wood is a dominant feature. Floorboards are made of oak and the walls lined with limed oak panelling, with a top rack for displaying Lady Nuffield's blue-and-white china. Further colour is provided by the Oriental rugs, a common feature throughout the house. See if you can spot the stains on the rugs; these were allegedly caused by Lady Nuffield's much-loved Scottie dogs.

Keeping time

Being a mechanical man Lord Nuffield had a fondness for clocks, which he liked to wind up and repair himself. There are many in the house, but particularly here in the hall, which features four English longcase clocks. By the front door is a 20th-century oak-cased clock which plays a choice of three tunes on tubular bells when chiming the quarters.

The great pretender

In the right company, Lord Nuffield enjoyed impersonating his favourite music hall artist, Albert Chevalier, whose sheet music and records you can see in this room. He would sometimes dress up as Chevalier and perform the singer's hit 'My Old Dutch' to the delight of his guests. Many commented on Lord Nuffield's fondness for singing and mimicry.

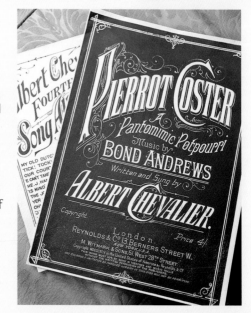

The Drawing Room

This was the best room of the house and as such only used when guests or family were visiting. Lady Nuffield would often go to Oxford on a Friday afternoon and return with cakes, which she would serve here to visitors at the weekend.

Sweet melodies

Music was a key part of the entertainments. Lord Nuffield had a large collection of records which included popular tunes of the day, music hall, operettas and some classical. Gilbert and Sullivan, Gracie Fields and Albert Chevalier were firm favourites. His HMV Superhet Ten radiogram with automatic record changer would have been state-of-the-art when it was acquired in the 1930s. The radiogram's instruction booklet is inscribed with annotations by Lord Nuffield.

Art Deco artefacts

On the nest of tables is a pair of stylish and ingenious 'Pullmatch' stands in silver with marble ashtrays. One pull on a red match would light it automatically. There are two eye-catching Art Deco clocks in the room – one sits on the mantelpiece, while the other hangs on the wall and features a mirrored sunburst, a typical Art Deco motif. The electric candlelights with wax drips are also a classic 1930s feature.

Much of the rest of the furniture in the room is reproduction, including the elegant Queen Anne-style walnut cabinet. Made by George Hughes Jr, it took 276 man-hours to make. The furniture may have been contemporary and reproduction, but it was of the best quality.

Above left The Sitting Room

Above right Lord Nuffield's HMV Superhet Ten radiogram with automatic record changer; notice the small needle boxes on the side

Opposite The Art Deco sunburst clock and ceramic parrots make a striking combination in the Drawing Room

The Dining Room

Like the Drawing Room, the Dining Room was only used for entertaining. Dinner guests would have included Sir Kennerly Rumford and his wife Dame Clara Butt, both famous singers, and Lady Nuffield's friend and neighbour, Mrs McKenzie, with whom she regularly walked her dogs.

The room was extended by the Nuffields to incorporate the original loggia which was at the French window end and the couple also introduced up-to-the-minute recessed strip lighting which added a sense of warmth and cosiness.

As elsewhere in the house much of the furniture, though seemingly antique, is reproduction. The 16th-century-style oak refectory table was made by Hallidays of Oxford, and so too were the tapestry dining chairs, though their designs came from Harrods. The tapestries are thought to be by Lee Tapestries of Birkenhead, whose founder, Arthur Lee (1853–1932), invented the process of hand block printing of colour designs onto woollen fabric. Examples of his work can be seen at Clarence House in London.

Classic prints

The Dining Room features one of the most popular series of prints ever created. Exhibited at the Royal Academy between 1792 and 1795, the *Cries of London* by Francis Wheatley RA is a set of 13 oil paintings representing different types of Covent Garden hawkers, such as the cherry seller, match seller, primrose seller, ballad seller, turnip seller and knife grinder. Through the 18th and 19th centuries the paintings were successfully reproduced and sold as prints. You may notice a similarity in the female figures, all of whom are allegedly based on Wheatley's wife.

Staff secrets

Food at Nuffield Place was usually cooked by Kathleen Francis, the housekeeper, though when there was to be a very fine dinner party, caterers were called in and Lady Nuffield would lay the table herself. During the meal, she would use the concealed Bakelite bell under the table to summon her staff.

Left The dining table set for dinner

Opposite The tapestry design on the Dining Room chairs was specially commissioned from Harrods

THE "CONA" COFFEE MACHINE

British made

OBTAINABLE AT ALL THE BEST STORES.

Quirky coffee

On the sideboard is a 1933 Cona coffee-maker. Unlike most other coffee machines, this one allowed you to make coffee at the table, creating a social ritual akin to tea-making in the 17th and 18th centuries. A stylish example of 1930s modernism, the same coffee maker can be spotted in the film *Brief Encounter*. Next to it sits an elegant 1930s chrome toaster – here form has clearly come before function as you can only toast one slice at a time!

The Sitting Room

This relatively small and intimate space was the everyday living room for Lord and Lady Nuffield. As such, it tells us much about them. You can imagine them sitting here in the evenings – he in his favourite wing armchair smoking and listening to the wireless (or, after 1955, watching TV); she sewing, writing a letter or filling her diary, with her Scottie dogs asleep by the fire.

Where there's smoke…

The Sitting Room contains many items relating to Lord Nuffield's smoking habit. Many of his portraits show him smoking, either a cigarette, cigar or a pipe. Note the song sheet on the chair entitled 'Song for Smokers' and the smoking paraphernalia in the cabinet. Fashionable at the time and originally used as a decorative device throughout the house, the gold ragwork ceiling was the ideal choice for the home of a smoker, acting as a perfect foil for nicotine stains.

When in the company of friends, Nuffield would sometimes throw a cigarette onto the carpet to scare them into thinking it would set fire. He would then laugh and explain that his cigarettes were specially made without any saltpetre and immediately went out when dropped. Such a picture is far removed from the image one might have of Lord Nuffield the successful businessman, and yet it is equally revealing of the man.

Lady Nuffield wrote many of her letters and diary entries at this desk

Beloved Scotties

On top of the wireless and in other parts of the room are models and pictures of Scottish terriers, a popular breed during the 1930s. Particularly attractive is the painting of four such dogs by German artist Meta Pluckebaum (1875–1945), who was famous for her portraits of children and animals. Lord and Lady Nuffield had three Scotties at one point. For a childless couple, one can imagine how these pets must have been more than a little indulged.

Personal gift

This Royal Worcester sphere was made for Lord Nuffield as a gift to thank him for his large donation to the Worcester Royal Infirmary. It is a reminder that as a child Lord Nuffield used to play marbles with a grinding ball from the Worcester porcelain factories. This he eventually lost in the canal behind his house, so the gift was offered as a 'replacement'. You can see a real grinding ball in the Delft bowl on the mantelpiece.

Morris mania

Lord Nuffield enjoyed collecting photos and portraits of people named Morris, even though none of them was a relative. Some of these can be seen in this room. The one of the doctor must have pleased Nuffield a lot, as he always wanted to join the medical profession.

Above Wireless and television in the Sitting Room; the HMV television was bought in 1955 and cost 105 guineas

Opposite Lord Nuffield was a keen smoker and also enjoyed a tipple

The Landing
The Single Guest Bedroom
Lady Nuffield's Bedroom

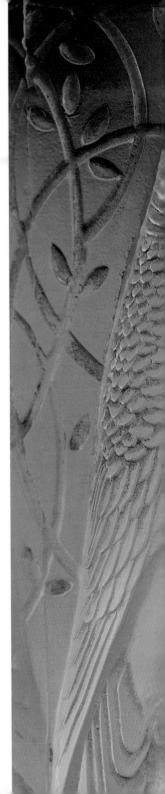

The Landing

Much like the Hall, the Landing features limed oak panelled doors and reproduction furniture. The unusual 'portrait' vase may have been a gift from his staff at the Cowley factory and hence features the MG and Morris badges. On the table are scrolls displaying some of the many honours Lord Nuffield received. The most interesting item, though, is the framed print honouring Lord Nuffield with the Freedom of the City of Coventry. He was presented with it on the day of Edward VIII's abdication, so the calligrapher had to cross out the wording referring to the King and add an explanatory note at the bottom. It is a fascinating historical document.

The Single Guest Bedroom

Decorated in yellow chintz, this room has been dressed as though a lady guest has just arrived and dropped off her suitcase and fur coat. The delicate lamp on the bedside table is by the French glass designer René Lalique. His work was particularly prized during the Art Deco era and may well have been collected by Lady Nuffield.

Odd artefacts

The policeman's truncheon hanging on the fire screen shows how Lady Nuffield was never able to relax at home after a borstal was established nearby after the Second World War. On the mantelpiece is a wartime shell case, a reminder that Morris Motors made munitions during the two wars.

Lady Nuffield's Bedroom

This is a feminine room adorned with flower and bird pictures and china ornaments. In the mornings, Lady Nuffield would sit in bed reading the paper while her husband did the same in his room. While she read the news, she would sometimes call him from her bedroom, and say, referring to his philanthropy: 'William, I have pencilled in something you should help.'

A photograph from 1963 shows that the bed was originally placed at an angle, possibly so that Lady Nuffield could enjoy the view

Left The Single Guest Bedroom

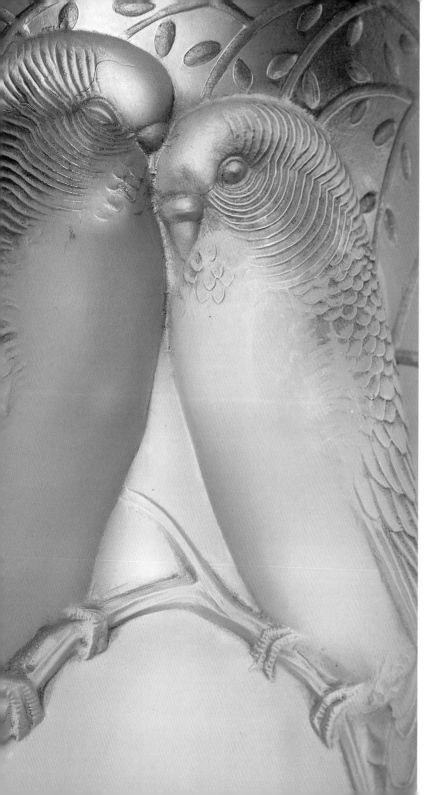

towards Wittenham Clumps, a small group of wooded hills in the otherwise flat Thames Valley. The photograph also shows a leopard skin rug on the floor. As we shall see, this was in stark contrast to the floor covering in Lord Nuffield's bedroom.

Delicate beauty

Lady Nuffield had her walnut suite specially made by Hallidays of Oxford. She insisted on it having dainty pull handles against the advice of the craftsman, who said that they would easily break. He was right, as you can see from the many missing handles. The green hand-painted table is part of a bedroom suite owned by the Morrises before they moved to Nuffield. It is in the style of Syrie Maugham, wife of Somerset Maugham, who was a fashionable interior designer in the 1930s. The footstool accompanying the chintz armchair was probably embroidered by Lady Nuffield.

Left Detail from a Lalique Art Deco lamp; budgerigars were a popular decorative motif in the 1930s

Above Lady Nuffield's bedroom, as it looked shortly after the house was bequeathed to Nuffield College

The Sun Room
Lord Nuffield's Bedroom

Rays of sunshine

On hot summer nights, Lord Nuffield would sleep in his Sun Room with the windows wide open. This was a time when people really believed in the health-giving benefits of fresh air, daylight and sunshine. It is therefore fitting that this room also features an ultra-violet lamp of the type Lord Nuffield presented to RAF Nightfighter stations and assembly-line workers during the Second World War to compensate for the sunlight deprivations they suffered.

Lord Nuffield's Bedroom

Lord Nuffield's true personality is revealed in his bedroom. Filled with practical items and basic furniture, it tells of a man who didn't believe in artifice or showiness. His simple bed was placed against the blocked-up fireplace, which acted as a headboard. Over the bed is a tangle of wires leading to a reading light, rigged up by Lord Nuffield himself. The floor is covered, not with expensive rugs, but with pieces of sewn-together carpet designed for the interiors of his cars.

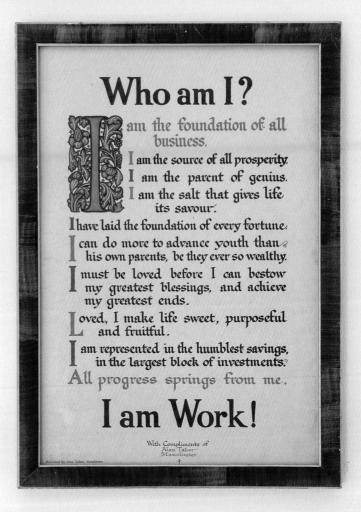

Who am I?

I am the foundation of all business.

I am the source of all prosperity.

I am the parent of genius.

I am the salt that gives life its savour.

I have laid the foundation of every fortune.

I can do more to advance youth than his own parents, be they ever so wealthy.

I must be loved before I can bestow my greatest blessings, and achieve my greatest ends.

Loved, I make life sweet, purposeful and fruitful.

I am represented in the humblest savings, in the largest block of investments.

All progress springs from me.

I am Work!

With Compliments of
Alan Tabor
Manchester

Published by Alan Tabor, Manchester

Curious cabinet

When Lord Nuffield couldn't sleep, he would occupy himself with mechanical work, which explains why an unusual mini-workshop is located in his bedroom. Amongst the well-used spanners, screwdrivers, saws, files, pliers and pincers are a number of more unexpected items, including packets of Phillips stick-on soles, a hooded torch from the Second World War, a mechanical toy bear, and Lord Nuffield's pickled appendix, which acts as a visual reminder of his interest in medicine.

Above Work was at the core of Lord Nuffield's life, as is made obvious by this framed poem in the Sun Room

Opposite This extraordinary workshop was a source of solace and occupation during Lord Nuffield's many sleepless nights

Pain-free operations

Someone once said to Lord Nuffield: 'Any fool can give an anaesthetic.' Having experienced a bad anaesthetic during a tooth operation, he was not of that opinion. And, inspired by the pain-free removal of his appendix by Dr Robert Macintosh, Nuffield set out to make anaesthetics a recognised subject within the field of medicine. In 1936 when the University of Oxford approached him to consider endowing three chairs in medicine, surgery and obstetrics, he insisted on adding a chair in anaesthetics, to be held by Macintosh. In 1937 Macintosh become the first professor of anaesthetics outside America; the event is commemorated by a plaque above Lord Nuffield's bed. Macintosh went on to develop special anaesthesia-related equipment and travelled widely, giving demonstrations of what he called 'safe and simple anaesthesia'.

Right Lord Nuffield's sparsely furnished bedroom reveals much about his passions and priorities

The bathrooms
Lady Nuffield's Sewing Room

Lady Nuffield's Sewing Room

Having trained as a seamstress at Elliston and Cavell, a department store in Oxford (now Debenhams), Lady Nuffield loved sewing. It was in this room that she made many of her own clothes, as well as uniforms for her staff.

The large cigar box and its contents are Lady Nuffield's original sewing box. She made the little pink dress when she was a girl at St Barnabas School in Oxford. The lady in the crinoline dress is also her creation. Intended as a tea cosy, this type of model was very popular in the 1930s.

Fine needlework

As well as sewing, Lady Nuffield also enjoyed tapestry work and many of the tapestry pieces in the house were made by her, although we do not know precisely which ones. She also enjoyed collecting tapestry pictures such as the fine Berlin woolwork pieces on the Landing, and also the samplers on the Landing, in Lady Nuffield's Dressing Room and in the Double Guest Bedroom.

The bathrooms

Unlike any other room in the house, the bathrooms are pure Art Deco. The Main Bathroom has marbled tiles by Carter's Industrial Tile Factory of Poole – later to become more famously known as Poole Pottery. The Carter company was responsible for manufacturing most of the tiles used in London Underground stations built in the 1930s. The room was originally painted in green-and-cream mottled-effect ragwork to match the tiles, while the yellow bathroom suite with chromium-plated mirror, taps and towel rail is typical of the streamlined 1930s look.

As was to be expected for a house of its time and size, every room featured a bell for calling the maid – but in this room the bell is positioned so that you can actually call her from the comfort of your bath!

Left Lady Nuffield's sewing box

Above One of the Art Deco bathrooms, featuring Poole Pottery tiles

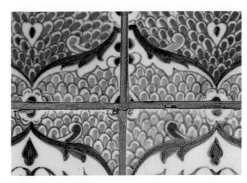

Mystery fireplace

The fireplace has a set of tiles from when the house was built in 1914. These were believed to be by the potter and tile designer William de Morgan, but recent research has established that they are not by him. The cobalt blue colour and flowing Art Nouveau curves are certainly reminiscent of his work.

The Double Guest Bedroom

Spacious and with a large bay window, this bedroom feels more luxurious than the other ones upstairs.

Honoured guests

The anaesthetist Sir Robert Macintosh (see page 23) and his wife Dorothy – both good friends of the Nuffields – may have stayed in this room, which has been dressed as if a couple were staying there and preparing for dinner. Notice the lady's gold evening dress and snakeskin shoes – maybe she will check how she looks in the cheval mirror.

Her suitcase has been left with her corset and her crepe stockings on show. The gentleman has placed his loose change on the bedside cabinet. When they go to bed the couple will enjoy the luxury of fine linen sheets, soft mattresses and quilted silk eiderdowns. They also have their own guest bathroom and lavatory.

All in the detail

As elsewhere in the house, this room is peppered with interesting items, which are revealing both of the Nuffields and of the

times in which they lived. Notice how the towel stand holds two towels with the initial 'N' for Nuffield – there are sets of other similar towels throughout the house. The large linen cupboard houses a collection of tablecloths, tray cloths and placemats, many of which were embroidered by Lady Nuffield. The moth-proofed dress covers on the door are part of a set designed to fit a canvas travelling wardrobe belonging to Lady Nuffield. The Oriental embroideries and pictures on the walls and mantelpiece were very fashionable in the 1930s, hence their appearance here and elsewhere in the house.

Gazunder

The bedside cupboard – part of the eight-piece walnut bedroom suite – has been designed to hold a chamber pot. This location is certainly a touch classier and more discreet than the usual under-the-bed placement of the ubiquitous chamber pot, from which its nickname 'gazunder' ('goes-under') originates.

Memory corner

On your way out, you can enjoy handling objects from when Lord and Lady Nuffield lived here. Children will like having a go at playing a record or dialling an old-fashioned telephone, while you can dress up in some of the clothes of the time, including stunning replica coronation robes.

Opposite Somewhat surprisingly, the Double Guest Bedroom is the largest bedroom in the house

Left Detail of oriental design on the fireguard

Above Embroidered towels in the Double Guest Bedroom

The Garden

The four-acre garden was originally designed by the architect of
the house, Oswald Milne, and laid out just after the First World
War. It combines lawns, herbaceous borders, yew hedges,
a pergola and a rock garden. The estate covers 9.2 acres, including
a wildflower meadow, vegetable garden and woodland.

Keen gardeners

Both Lady and Lord Nuffield loved their garden. She would spend hours in old clothes and gardening boots tending her flowers, while he enjoyed doing odd jobs outdoors. Three full-time gardeners looked after the plot under the supervision of the 'gardener-in-chief', Lady Nuffield. The kitchen garden provided the house with fresh vegetables and fruit, some of which she would bottle or make into jam.

The Rose Garden

Beds filled entirely with roses were a typical feature of mid-20th-century gardens. By the 1980s, however, the roses here had been replaced by herbaceous perennials, partly due to damage caused by deer nibbling the rose buds. The plan is to recreate the Rose Garden to echo its original design.

The Rose Walk

The paved Rose Walk, originally topped with a long rose-clad pergola, leads you to the Lower Lawn. The undulating yew hedges either side are part of Milne's design. Being evergreen, they make an attractive winter feature. A new pergola, based on the original design, will soon be in place.

The Lower Lawn

As you go down some steps and through an iron gate, you enter a large area of lawn framed by tall trees, which in their heyday were so many and various that they formed a mini-arboretum. From the Lower Lawn you can enjoy a good view of the house, with its charming blue shutters. On its wall is a striking vertical sundial, whose Roman numerals II to IX show the time when the sun's rays touch that side of the house. The sundial was the creation of Macdonald Gill, brother of the sculptor and typeface designer Eric Gill.

Wonderful woodland

As you walk southwards, the foreground of specimen conifers soon gives way to a copse of beech and oak trees, known as the Bluebell Woodland because of its abundance of bluebells in late spring. The path eventually leads to a children's play area, although there are also a couple of left turns along the way which can take you back into the main garden.

Above top Lord Nuffield in his garden, 1962

Above The rustic hut near the Bluebell Woodland

Opposite The Rose Garden as it looks today, filled with an assortment of perennials

Above This allée of trees was situated near the Herbaceous Border (see page 30)

The Tennis Court Lawn

The lawn on the south side of the house served as an occasional tennis court; more recently it has been home to games of croquet. The dry-stone wall to its left was added by Lord and Lady Nuffield, replacing Milne's original brick wall. During the 1920s and 30s there was a craze for alpine and rock gardens, and we have photographic evidence that the wall did indeed feature such plants.

The Herbaceous Border

Very early photographs show this west-facing border planted with standard roses and bedding plants, such as antirrhinums. Photos from the 1950s, however, reveal a 'cottage garden' style of planting, with irises, lupins and delphiniums in shades of yellow, orange and blue. It seems likely that this more informal and fashionable style was adopted by the Nuffields when they moved here in the 1930s. The border is currently (2013) undergoing restoration.

The Rock Garden

Part of the original garden design, the Rock Garden would have consisted mostly of low-growing flowering alpine and rock plants, though photographs from the 1940s and 1950s show the increasing dominance of shrubs such as heathers and conifers. By the end of the

Below Delicate depiction of a classic 1930s rock garden by Lilian Stannard (1877–1944)

Through the opening in the brick-and-flint wall were greenhouses which contained tender plants and provided out-of-season flowers and fruit for the house. One of the original greenhouses is still in place and has recently been restored. It now offers a useful propagation and over-wintering area. The nearby garage with attractive wooden tower was built in 1933–4; it is now home to Lady Nuffield's Wolseley.

Mind the gate

Lord Nuffield had special hydraulic pads fitted on each side of the entrance gates to Nuffield Place; as the weight of the car pressed down the gates would open and close automatically. This mechanism was a source of great amusement to children in the village, who would go down in groups to 'jump on the pads' and make the gates open. On one such occasion Lord Nuffield, hid behind the bushes and sprang out to surprise the children!

Above Lady Nuffield in her garden

20th century, the planting had become patchy, and weeds and other self-sown plants had taken over. The Rock Garden is now being restored, a process which has involved the removal of all plants, as well as the top soil. After a fallow period of at least a year, it will hopefully be clear of any perennial and invasive weeds, such as horsetail (*Equisetum arvense*). The garden will then be filled with a mix of loam and grit and replanted with a variety of alpines and rock plants.

The North Garden

On the north side of the house are brick-edged island beds cut through by small paths and planted with woodland and shade-loving plants including hellebores, geraniums, ferns and foxgloves.

Staff at Nuffield

Lord and Lady Nuffield relied on a housekeeper, one or two
maids and a cleaner to help with the running of their house.

untrusting and overbearing. She was fond of
Lord Nuffield though and remembers how he
would sometimes dip into his pocket and press
a pound note into her hand, saying: 'Quick, put
this out of sight, it's for your mother.'

A few other live-in maids left after a short
while but the housekeeper, Kathleen, stayed
for 30 years between 1933 and 1963 – so maybe
things were not as bad as Ivy remembers. In
recognition of her work, Lord Nuffield left a
small legacy to Kathleen.

Left The loyal housekeeper,
Kathleen Francis

Below The maid would
have done some cleaning
and polishing in the Pantry,
which also acted as a store
room. Today, it contains
kitchen items from the
Nuffields' time

In 1935 Ivy Vernon, aged 14, became the maid at
Nuffield Place. Her memories give us little clues
as to what it was like to work here. At the time,
there were two other domestic servants:
Kathleen Francis did the cooking and was Lady
Nuffield's personal maid, and Dorothy Sellars,
the gardener's wife, did most of the cleaning.

Ivy slept in a small room on the top floor.
She started work at 6am and finished at around
10pm every day with no regular day off. She
didn't like working here and left after just a
year. This was mainly because she did not get
on with Lady Nuffield, whom she saw as mean,